Investing

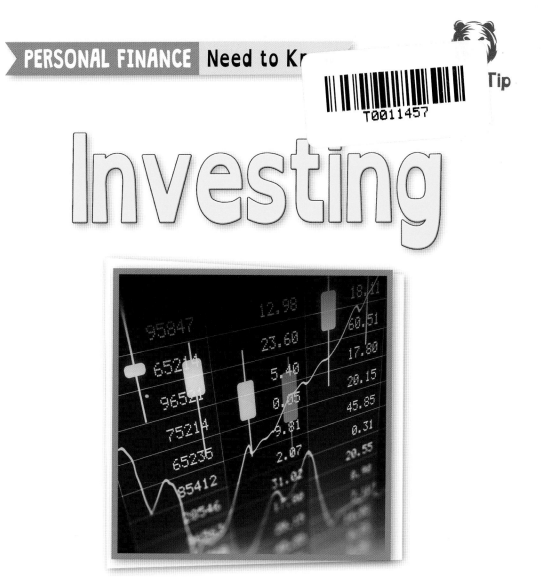

by Ruth Owen

Consultant: Kari Servais
Middle School Family & Consumer Science Educator

BEARPORT
PUBLISHING

Minneapolis, Minnesota

Credits

Cover and title page, © cemagraphics/iStock; 5, © Luis Molinero/Shutterstock; 7, © Gorodenkoff/Shutterstock; 9, © Ryan DeBerardinis/Shutterstock; 11, © FinancePix/Alamy; 13, © lammotos/Shutterstock; 15, © Kaspars Grinvalds/Shutterstock; 16–17, © sitox/Getty Images; 19, © lunamarina/Shutterstock; 20–21, © Jonathan Weiss/Shutterstock; 23, © Ronald Sumners/Shutterstock; 24–25, © Mikhail Markovskiy/Shutterstock; and 27, © Lopolo/Shutterstock.

Bearport Publishing Company Product Development Team

President: Jen Jenson; Director of Product Development: Spencer Brinker; Senior Editor: Allison Juda; Editor: Charly Haley; Associate Editor: Naomi Reich; Senior Designer: Colin O'Dea; Associate Designer: Elena Klinkner; Associate Designer: Kayla Eggert; Product Development Assistant: Anita Stasson

Library of Congress Cataloging-in-Publication Data

Names: Owen, Ruth, 1967– author.
Title: Investing / Ruth Owen.
Description: Minneapolis, Minnesota : Bearport Publishing Company, [2023] |
   Series: Personal finance: need to know | Includes bibliographical
   references and index.
Identifiers: LCCN 2022039488 (print) | LCCN 2022039489 (ebook) | ISBN
   9798885094160 (library binding) | ISBN 9798885095389 (paperback) | ISBN
   9798885096539 (ebook)
Subjects: LCSH: Investments–Juvenile literature. | Finance,
   Personal–Juvenile literature. | Money–Juvenile literature.
Classification: LCC HG4521 .O94 2023 (print) | LCC HG4521 (ebook) | DDC
   332.67/8–dc23/eng/20220923
LC record available at https://lccn.loc.gov/2022039488
LC ebook record available at https://lccn.loc.gov/2022039489

For more information, write to Bearport Publishing, 5357 Penn Avenue South, Minneapolis, MN 55419.

Contents

Make Money with Your Money 4

What Is Investing? 6

At the Market 8

Time to Share 12

When Stocks Go Up! 14

The Downside 18

Buying Bonds. 20

Join the Crowd. 22

Be a Smart Investor. 24

Get Ready for the Future. 26

Be an Investor. 28

SilverTips for Success 29

Glossary 30

Read More 31

Learn More Online 31

Index 32

About the Author. 32

Make Money with Your Money

If you get money for your birthday, what do you do? You might spend it right away or save it for another time. But you can also use your money to make more money. How does this work? It can happen when you're **investing**.

Investing isn't the only way to grow money. If you put cash into a savings account, it makes a little extra money called **interest**.

What Is Investing?

When you invest money, you give it to a company in the hope of getting more back later. A company uses this money to run its business. If the company does well, investors can make back their money plus some extra. But if the company does poorly, investors can lose money.

Some people invest small amounts of money. Others invest a lot. This can depend on how much money a person has and how much they think they'll get from the investment.

At the Market

One main way people invest is by buying **stocks**. A stock is a small part, or share, of a company. Investors buy stocks through a **stock market**. Some people invest in companies that sell products they like. Many investors buy stocks in companies they think will do well.

People can make a lot of money from stocks. But these investments are risky, too. Sometimes, people lose some or all of the money they invest.

The New York Stock Exchange building holds a big stock market.

Many countries have a stock market. In the United States, the main stock market is in New York City. People called **traders** buy and sell stocks for investors. In just one day, they trade billions of dollars worth of stocks.

Traders can help investors make smart choices with their money. But some people do not use a trader to buy and sell stocks. Instead, they invest in stocks online by themselves.

Time to Share

When a person buys a stock in a company, they become a **shareholder**. Someone who buys lots of stocks in one company owns a larger share than someone with fewer stocks. Shareholders may have a say in what the company does.

People with more shares may have more of a voice in a company. Sometimes, the biggest shareholders get to vote on important decisions.

When Stocks Go Up!

How do investors make money from stocks? It happens when a company they invest in is successful. All companies hope to make a **profit**. They want to take in more money than they spend. This success makes the **value** of the company's stocks go up. Then, each share is worth more money.

Let's say an investor buys a stock for $25. The company does well, and the stock's value goes up to $50. Now, the stock is worth twice as much as what the investor paid for it!

As stocks change value, shareholders decide whether to keep or sell their stocks. If an investor chooses to sell their stocks after the value goes up, they can make a profit. But if they decide to keep their shares, the value may go up even more.

If a company is doing well, it may pay its shareholders an amount of money for each share they own. These one-time payments are called **dividends**. They are another way for investors to make money from stocks.

The Downside

Investors take a chance on whether a company will be successful. If a company is not making a profit, the value of its stocks goes down. The value also goes down if people don't like a company and don't want its stocks. This can happen when a company does something bad.

When stocks go down, investors might keep their shares and hope the value goes back up. Or they might decide to sell and lose some money.

Buying Bonds

Another way people can invest is to buy **bonds** from a company or the government. Unlike stocks, bonds are not tied to how well a company does. They are a way for investors to lend their money with the promise of having it all paid back plus interest.

Buying bonds from the government is a safe way to invest. The government guarantees you will not lose your money. Companies do not make the same promise with stocks.

Join the Crowd

Looking for a fun way to invest in things you like? Try crowdfunding. This is when people ask for money to support their projects. Each person who gives money is an investor. They often get something back. For example, when investors help fund a band's album, they may get a free copy in return.

Crowdfunding websites let people invest in almost anything. People can give money to businesses making new video games, board games, books, movies, or cool gadgets.

Be a Smart Investor

Some investments are more risky than others. An investor can reduce their own risk by having different kinds of investments. This is called **diversification** (di-*vur*-si-fi-KAY-shun). It could mean having both stocks and bonds. It could also be having stocks in several companies. If the value of some goes down, hopefully others go up.

When the stock market is doing well, most stock values rise. This is called a bull market. When most stock values are going down, it's a bear market.

Get Ready for the Future

Investing can be full of ups and downs. The longer you stick with it, the more likely you are to make money. Smart investing can help you with long-term goals, such as buying a car. The key is waiting through the lows to get to the highs.

Investing is often better for long-term goals. You may lose money in the short-term. However, over a long period, most investments make money.

Be an Investor

How might someone make money from their investments? Let's see how someone could invest $2,500.

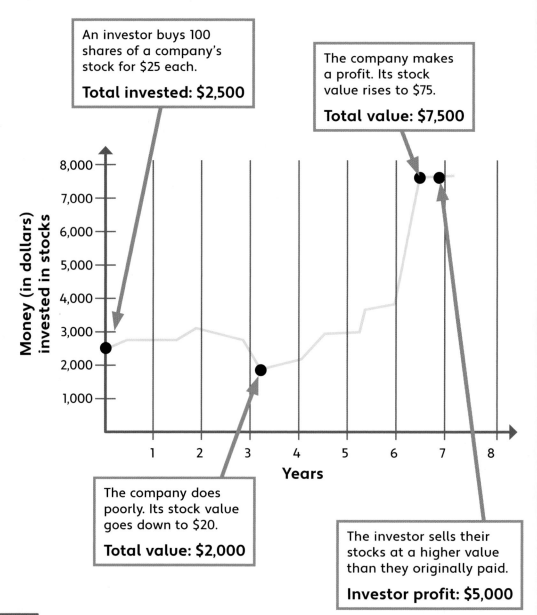

An investor buys 100 shares of a company's stock for $25 each.

Total invested: $2,500

The company makes a profit. Its stock value rises to $75.

Total value: $7,500

The company does poorly. Its stock value goes down to $20.

Total value: $2,000

The investor sells their stocks at a higher value than they originally paid.

Investor profit: $5,000

Y-axis: Money (in dollars) invested in stocks — 1,000; 2,000; 3,000; 4,000; 5,000; 6,000; 7,000; 8,000

X-axis: Years — 1, 2, 3, 4, 5, 6, 7, 8

★ SilverTips for REVIEW

Review what you've learned. Use the text to help you.

Define key terms

bonds   shareholder

investing   stocks

profit

Check for understanding

What is the difference between stocks and bonds?

How do investors make money from stocks?

Why is diversification a good idea?

Think deeper

Why would someone want to invest in stocks, bonds, or crowdfunding? Why not?

★ SilverTips on TEST-TAKING

- **Make a study plan.** Ask your teacher what the test is going to cover. Then, set aside time to study a little bit every day.

- **Read all the questions carefully.** Be sure you know what is being asked.

- **Skip any questions** you don't know how to answer right away. Mark them and come back later if you have time.

Glossary

bonds loans to a company or government that earn interest for the lender

diversification the act of separating invested money into different places

dividends payments to shareholders when a company makes a profit

interest money in addition to an amount in a bank account or used for a loan

investing spending money with the goal of getting more money back

profit the amount of money left after all related costs have been paid

shareholder a person who owns stocks in a company

stock market a place where stocks are bought and sold

stocks parts of a company that can be bought and sold

traders people whose job is to invest in the stock market

value the amount of money that something is worth

Read More

Fiedler, Heidi. *The Know-Nonsense Guide to Money: An Awesomely Fun Guide to the World of Finance! (Know Nonsense Series).* Mission Viejo, CA: Walter Foster Jr., 2022.

Hill, Christina. *The Stock Market in Infographics (Econo-graphics).* Ann Arbor, MI: Cherry Lake Press, 2023.

London, Martha. *Saving and Investing (Money Basics).* San Diego, CA: BrightPoint Press, 2020.

Learn More Online

1. Go to **www.factsurfer.com** or scan the QR code below.

2. Enter "**Investing**" into the search box.

3. Click on the cover of this book to see a list of websites.

Index

bonds 20, 24

crowdfunding 22

diversification 24

dividends 17

interest 4, 20

New York Stock Exchange 9

profit 14, 16, 18, 28

risk 8, 24

saving 4

shareholders 12, 16–17

stock market 8–11, 25

stocks 8–12, 14, 16–18, 20, 24–25, 28

traders 10–11

About the Author

Ruth Owen has written hundreds of non-fiction books. She lives on the Cornish coast in England with her husband and three cats.